The Devil is Winning

Because You're Not Walking in Your Power

Raine Cunningham

The Proverbial Seed

© 2025 Raine Cunningham

All rights reserved.

No part of this publication may be reproduced, distributed, or transmitted in any form or by any means, including photocopying, recording, or other electronic or mechanical methods, without the prior written permission of the publisher. Exception is granted in the case of brief quotations embodied in critical reviews and certain other non-commercial uses permitted by copyright law.

To my grandmother, Lucille Bellamy
Thank you for planting boldness in me
long before I knew I would need it.
You lived with courage, honesty, and a fire
that still burns in my spirit.
You left this world too soon,
but the seeds you planted live on, in me,
and in all who will be touched by these words.

Author's Note

This book was born from a journey, not just of survival, but of spiritual reclamation. At its heart is the belief that truth, when internalized, can transform how we see ourselves, our past, and our purpose.

In crafting this series, I've drawn from the teachings of **Neville Goddard**, whose work on *imagination* and *the power of consciousness* has reshaped my understanding of faith and agency. Alongside him, the poetic and prophetic voice of **William Blake** stirred something deep in me...a reminder that the spiritual and the symbolic are intertwined.

You'll also see threads of the **Bible** woven throughout these pages, not as dogma, but as living dialogue. I honor its sacred text as both a record of divine truth and a mirror through which we confront, challenge, and reclaim our identity.

This book is an invitation to revisit *your* life with new eyes, to reclaim what is yours, and to boldly share your -self with the world through your purpose.

With love and truth,
Raine Cunningham

About Goddard and Blake

Neville Goddard

Neville Goddard (1905–1972) was a spiritual teacher and author whose writings on imagination, faith, and the creative power of thought continue to inspire seekers around the world. His teachings emphasize that what we imagine and believe shape our reality...a truth that resonates throughout *The Power Reclaimed book series*.

William Blake

William Blake (1757–1827) was an English poet, artist, and visionary whose works wove together imagination and spiritual symbolism. Sometimes controversial, Blake's fearless exploration of the seen and unseen world lends a timeless depth to the call of this book...to see beyond the surface and reclaim a higher truth.

Introduction

Permission to Be Powerful

You've been waiting for permission.

This is not a self-help book. This is a *spiritual intervention*.

You didn't choose this book by accident. You were led here by divine dissatisfaction, the kind that whispers, *"There's more to life than this."*

You've been sensing it. That strange discomfort. The tension between who you are and who you're called to be. Then there's the question that won't stop echoing..."*Why does it feel like the enemy keeps winning?"*

Not just in your home. Not just about your purpose. But in your heart. In your decisions. In your silence. In your delay.

Understand that the devil isn't winning because *he's* powerful. He's winning because you've been convinced that *you are not*.

You've been restrained by fear. Stalled by confusion. Wrapped in false humility. Distracted by survival.

And all the while, your power has been lying dormant inside of you, waiting to be reclaimed.

"The Devil is Winning..." was not written from a pulpit...no stage...no sold-out arena. It was written from a wilderness. From experience. From pain. From the trenches of spiritual identity. From my own divine wrestle.

This book is not here to provide you with steps...it's here to hand you a mirror and to let you know that you are not powerless. You never were. But you can't walk in what you won't claim.

You have permission to be powerful. You have permission to rise. You have permission to remember who you are.

The enemy doesn't get the final word...God does!

Contents

1. The Lie of Powerlessness — 1
2. When God Speaks, But You Remain Silent — 11
3. The Cycle of Delay — 21
4. Boldness Is Not Arrogance — 31
5. Obedience Is the First Weapon — 39
6. Authority in Your Atmosphere — 47
7. The Devil Only Wins When You Withdraw — 55
8. Power Reclaimed...in Real Life — 61
9. The Awakening — 67

Thank You — 73

About the Series — 75

About the author — 77

Chapter One

The Lie of Powerlessness

Who told you that you were powerless?

There is a war for your identity. The war doesn't begin in your relationships...not with your parents, your children, or your significant other.

The war doesn't even begin with any trauma you may have experienced.

The war begins in your *imagination*...otherwise, in your *thoughts*.

The most successful lie the devil ever told was that *you are not who God says you are.*

It feels like defeat. It sounds like exhaustion. It looks like procrastination. It moves like delay.

It's not loud. It's an almost silent whisper. But in your spirit, it roars.

It puts you in a trance...it renders you immobile...and it takes a *word* to shake you out of it.

The night I was shaken out of *my* spiritual *slumber* was not during a fast, or a revival...nor was it during any *other* spectacular event. No! It was late at night, and I was sitting alone, at my dining room table.

I had been promising myself for weeks that I would wash the dishes, and wow...they were piled up, yet...I kept putting it off.

Work had drained me. Thoughts of all the things I *should* have done that day had drained me. I guess I had drained myself. In my mind I was busy but I had nothing to show for it. Emotionally, I was done.

I sat there thinking I should already have been in the kitchen, trying to bring some kind of order to the mountain of dishes that lay before me. Instead, I was playing endless games of Hearts on my phone. Then, bored with that, I started scrolling through Instagram reels, then Facebook videos...mindless swiping...procrastination.

I glanced over at the clock. It was almost midnight...I had to work the next morning. I peeped over at the dishes again and *thought*, "guess I'll get at 'em tommorow".

In that instance, I heard a voice. Not in my ear. I heard it in my Spirit. It was quiet at first. I heard..."*The devil is winning because you're not walking in your power.*"

For a second, I couldn't move. I was frozen...not with fear...more like surprise. Then I heard it again, louder... *"the devil is winning because you are not walking in your power!"*

After that, the voice was even louder, and more stern, "*and you are not walking in your purpose, because you're not walking in your power!* Now get over there and wash the dishes!" It was definitely a reprimand.

I sat there for another minute or two, it could have been 10 seconds, but I was going over in my head, what I thought I heard. Then I obediently walked over to the kitchen, put the food away, and I washed the dishes. When I say nothing was left in the sink, on the counter, or on the stove; I mean I washed everything.

In that moment, for *me...deliverance* looked like *washing the dishes*. *Obedience* looked like me, standing in my kitchen, having victory over the very thing that, for *weeks*, I had not been able to muster the power to accomplish. Washing dishes!

That night, it felt like the Spirit of God had reclaimed ground in my soul. Reminding me who I was...whose I was...and what I was called to do.

The Forgotten "I AM"

Neville Goddard taught that *"I AM" is the name of God, and is man's forgotten identity.* "Until man discovers that 'I AM' is his -*self*, he will remain enslaved." Enslaved by fear. By trauma. By people-pleasing. By the illusion of being stuck.

When Moses asked God for His name, God replied: *"I AM THAT I AM."* (Exodus 3:14) When you say *"I am tired,"* you're not merely complaining, you are *creating*. When you say *"I am not enough,"* you are using the name of God to deny your divinity. I had spent too many days...too many nights, too much time saying...

~ I'm too tired to...

~ I'm too old to...

~ I'm too behind to...

But that night, at my table, then repeatedly while I was washing dishes, I was reminded: "I AM is *my* name." My *true* name. "I AM is my portal to power."

Mind-Forged Manacles

William Blake, in his prophetic work *Jerusalem*, wrote about the *"mind-forged manacles"*...invisible chains that imprison the human soul through *thought*.

I had been *chained* by childhood trauma. *Chained* by everything that comes with growing up in the inner city, and then some.

I had been *chained* by family cycles of dysfunction...and abuse.

I had been *chained* by emotional exhaustion, *masked* as strength. And I had been chained by a lifetime of putting everyone else first.

But Blake's message, and Goddard's interpretation, became clear. *"You must create your system or be enslaved by another man's."*

Through those chains, I had been living in *systems* I never agreed to. Systems of over-functioning. Systems of guilt. Systems of spiritual silence.

God was calling me to break *my* manacles...with a dish towel in my hand, and a *fire* in my spirit.

The lie of powerlessness had died. It was gone...just like that! And I *completely* understood.

The Lie That Hides in Plain Sight

Powerlessness doesn't always scream. Sometimes it sounds like...

~ *"I need a break."*

~ *"It's not the right time."*

~ *"I'm not ready."*

These are *not* random statements. These are *agreements*. And with whomever you agree, God or the enemy; with *whomever* you agree, gains access to you.

The devil doesn't need to destroy you. He just needs you to *withdraw*. To delay. To defer. To say "later", when God says "go now."

I've come to understand that hell only advances when you acutely *remember, and dwell on,* what you've been through, but you've forgotten who you are.

Memory Is a Weapon

I remember growing up in the midst of domestic violence, and suffering through discipline that is now considered child abuse.

I remember living in a multi-family apartment building, filled with both love and liquor. Good times and bad. Joy and pain.

I remember being hopelessly "in love"...stuck on stupid. And I remember the devastation of that break-up.

And I remember being told that I would never bear children...but losing one by miscarriage.

I remember, for so long, *not being carried*, because *I AM* the carrier. I remember life...often... being too much to bear.

Yet, I remember that God kept me every time. He kept me from people with ill intentions...and He keeps me from my own self-destruction.

What I realize, is that...every day I survive, is a sign that *I AM not powerless*...and *I AM not* forgotten...*I AM chosen*!

Reframe Your "I AM" Dialogue...

I AM not exhausted...I AM filled with fresh oil!

I AM not too late...I AM right on time for God's plan!

I AM not behind...I AM in divine alignment!

I AM not powerless...I AM called! I AM chosen!

I AM evidence of His goodness!

Reflections

What **lies** do you believe about who you are? Lies that keep your light from shining.

_____

_____

What "I AM..." **lies** do you speak to yourself, daily, that still have you broken and chained?

_____

_____

Who told you that you had to wait to be great? Or that you were too *this* or to *that* to win!

_____

_____

What would change if you started *every* day, knowing that you were powerful, not powerless?

_____

_____

Declarations

I AM not what I've been through.

I AM what God is doing next, through me.

I AM breaking chains.

I AM no longer available for defeat.

I AM not available for delay, or shame, or spiritual decay.

I AM walking in my power!

Notes

_____

_____

_____

_____

_____

_____

Chapter Two
When God Speaks, But You Remain Silent

Delayed obedience is disobedience

There are moments when God speaks, and everything in your spirit *knows* it's Him. You feel it in your belly. You feel it in your bones. You get excited. You log it in your journal. You *cry*. You *shout*, and do your little dance, because the *word* was *sooo* good. But then...you do nothing.

You sit with the instruction...the call. You over-analyze it. You file it under *'later'*. "I'll do it...later." Then *later*...you start to "pray about it", even though you *already* got the *word*. And somewhere between the revelation and the execution...you go silent. This chapter is especially for *you*. The one who hears God, and still won't move.

Silence Feels Safe

Silence isn't always neutral. Silence *can* be agreement. Silence can be delay. Silence can be a trauma response. I've known that silence.

There were times when I clearly heard God speak to me.

I heard Him when He told me to leave a relationship.

I heard him when He said to pursue an opportunity...a job...a house...a car, etc.

I heard Him when He told me to *tell my story*.

Sometimes He would say "*start over*", or "*rest*", or "*confront*", or "*trust*", or "*forgive*".

And I didn't move. Not because I didn't believe Him. I didn't move because the cost was too high.

The Inner Dialogue That Kills Destiny

We don't always say *no* to God out loud. Sometimes we say *no* in the quiet recesses of our mind. *No* is often played out as...

~ *What if I fail?*

~ *What if they think I'm crazy?*

~ *What if I misheard Him?*

~ *What if I'm not ready?*

~ *What if...?*

The truth is...**the moment you silence your obedience, you give way to your fear.** Fear is noisy. The voice of fear is loud...thunderous at times.

It stops you in your tracks. Only you can hear it, and it paralyzes you.

Partial Obedience Is Disobedience

In 1 Samuel 15, after God told Saul to destroy *everything*, he spared King Agag and the best of the livestock.

Saul was probably thinking "I did *most* of what I was told to do."

Samuel let him know that *"to obey is better than sacrifice."* (1 Samuel 15:22)

God doesn't just want our worship, He wants our *follow-through*. He wants our obedience.

And it's not about being perfect! Countless times I gave God praise in one breath, and gave Him hesitation in the next.

Not because I didn't trust Him, but because I didn't trust *myself* to carry what He gave me. I didn't believe that I was enough.

When You're Called, But You're Cautious

Most of the time, the issue isn't disbelief in God...it's disbelief in *yourself*. You know *He's* able. You know *He's* faithful.

But you're still waiting to feel *qualified* before you speak what He told you, or write what He gave you, or build what He showed you.

I didn't always trust my voice. I knew I had *some* wisdom. I knew I was given a *word...a command...an assignment*. But for decades, I hesitated to speak...because for as long as I could remember, I had been trained to be *silent*. Told to "speak only when spoken to".

I was taught to be strong, yet...be quiet! Be responsible, yet...be quiet!

Be in charge, yet...be quiet! Be confident, yet...be quiet!

Be all that you can be, yet...be quiet!

So when God said, *"Speak boldly"*, years of cultural, emotional, and spiritual, conditioning had to be broken before I could utter a word.

The Danger of Spiritual Suppression

Silence might feel safe, but it's also where *purpose* goes to die. You can be anointed and still be unavailable. You can be chosen and still be mute. And every time you stay silent, when God says speak, you yield territory. Not just for yourself, but for the people assigned to your voice.

It's not just about disobedience. It's about the interruption of legacy. When you stay silent, people who are waiting on your *yes*, get delayed.

God Speaks in Cycles, Not Just in Moments

Have you ever noticed that God will give you a word, a command...and then *His voice* gets quiet?

You hear nothing...for a while. You think He's turned away, or have forgotten you. No!

His silence...is your window of execution...*your* time to fulfill the command.

When God speaks, He expects movement. When you don't move, He will close the door on *that* opportunity because you sat there staring at the door, instead of walking through it.

Yes, some assignments do expire. When they do, you'll be out of sync for a while...out of alignment...and you'll feel it, but you'll be alright.

Days, weeks, months, and sometimes *years*, will pass and that *word, that command, that assignment, will* presents itself once again. The next time though, His *method of notification* will be different, and His *timing* will be different, but you'll recognize it, and you'll be ready.

Neville Goddard and the Power of Words

"Your word is your wand." -Neville Goddard

What you speak...and *don't* speak...creates your world. If *I AM* is the name of God, within you, then refusing to say what God told you to say, or do what He told you to do, is an act of spiritual self-denial.

Blake called it "turning away from Jerusalem"...the inner city of the soul, where you and God dwell in communion. When you stay silent, you're not just rejecting the assignment...you're turning away from *your -self, from your I AM*.

My Breaking Point

I had gotten to a place where my silence had become more painful than my fear. That moment came in the quiet. It came late at night, in a dimly lit dining room, as I glanced over at a sink full of dishes, and a countertop with just as many.

It was a quiet, still moment. It was a moment when God chastised me through my own spirit. When He said… *"the devil is winning because you are not walking in your power,* and *you're not walking in your purpose, because you are not walking in your power!"*

That was the last time I could take, or mis-take, my *silence* for being a place of safety.

Reflections

What has God told you to do that you've delayed?

_____

_____

What fears or conditions have kept you silent?

_____

_____

_____

Who or what are you waiting on to feel *ready*?

_____

_____

_____

What *one* act of obedience can you take *today* to break the silence?

_____

_____

_____

Declarations

I do not cower from the voice of God, I move in step with it.

I am not waiting for permission. I have already been sent.

Delayed obedience is still disobedience, and I choose alignment.

When God speaks, I respond with power, clarity, and faith.

Notes

_____

_____

_____

_____

_____

_____

_____

_____

Chapter Three
The Cycle of Delay
Just more disobedience

There is a delay that is divine and there is a delay that is *self-imposed*. Some delays protect you, others expose your reluctance. Some are God's timing…others are your avoidance strategy dressed in spiritual conversation.

This chapter is not about the delay God orchestrates. It's about the delay *you* perpetuate. The kind of delay you justify. The kind of delay you excuse. The kind of delay you've gotten so used to that it's now your rhythm.

It's time to break that cycle.

What is the Cycle of Delay?

The cycle of delay is a spiritual loop that keeps you busy, but not obedient. You hear God. You know what to do. You may even start...but you stop. You slow-walk the instruction. You over plan. You stutter. You hesitate.

Then time passes, and guilt enters. You say, *"I should have started already."* You start again, but the same fears, distractions, or voices creep in. You stop...again. And that becomes your cycle: *Start. Stall. Shame. Start again.*

Delay Feels Safe...Until It Doesn't

Delay can feel comforting. It gives you space to "prepare more," to "pray more," to "get more things in order." But too often, that preparation is a *delay* tactic in disguise.

The truth is...you're not afraid of failing. You're afraid of what success will *require*. You're afraid of who you'll lose. You're afraid of being seen.

Understand that delay becomes disobedience when it keeps you from your assignment. And eventually, the safety of delay turns into the stagnation of *purpose*.

What Delay Really Costs

Delay is expensive, and it costs you more than just time.

It costs you...

~ *Momentum*

~ *Confidence*

~ *Influence*

~ *Peace*

~ *Obedience*

...and it costs those who are waiting on you...

Your family continues to miss the fruit of your obedience

Your clients miss the breakthrough you were meant to deliver... in whatever industry

Your future -*self* misses alignment

There are people who need what you carry, but they're on the other side of your *yes*.

Mental Loops and Inner Delays

"Change your conception of your *-self* and you will automatically change the world in which you live." -Neville Goddard

If your inner conversation is laced with doubt, your *external life* will always reflect hesitation.

You delay sending that email because *you're afraid to sound too bold.*

You delay recording the video because *you don't like your voice.*

You delay applying to that position because *you're not sure you belong in the room.*

Remember...your *thought life* governs your timing. Delay doesn't start on your clock, or on your calendar. It starts in your *mind*. As Goddard taught, "your inner assumptions shape your outer reality".

When you *assume* delay, meaning when you practice disobedience. When you don't move when you're supposed to move, everything gets delayed.

Moses Delayed Himself

When God called Moses, he delayed. Moses argued. Hesitated. And gave excuses.

~ *Who am I to go?*

~ *What if they don't believe me?*

~ *I'm not a good speaker.*

God had to remind Moses... *"Who gave human beings their mouths? Is it not I, the Lord?"* (Exodus 4:11)

And yet Moses still begged, *"Please send someone else."*

Many of us, like Moses, are more confident in our *weakness* than in God's *assignment*. So we delay. We avoid. We disqualify ourselves before we even start.

My Delay Nearly Cost Me My Voice

I know this cycle *too* well. It was the epitome of who I was.

People would tell me that I should be a nurse, or that I should teach, or that I should write a book.

I sat for years with *ideas*...outlines for greatness.

While life happened around me, God breathed countless opportunities. Many ideas were dropped in my spirit. They were opportunities for me to *walk in my purpose.*

Most of the time, I was consumed with family, friends, work, illness, disappointment, exhaustion, and fear. Excuses!

I kept telling myself, o*ne day I'll finish it.* What was *it? It* could have been any one of the many projects I had started. *One day I'll get to it.*

Basically, I was saying...*one day I'll obey.*

Delay doesn't just cost you *time*. It can cost you your *momentum*, your *credibility*, your *fire*. The worst part is you begin to normalize your silence. You forget what it feels like to *move on time.*

I am *constantly* reminded of my Awakening...when the Spirit chastised me by saying... *"the devil is winning because you are not walking in your power, and you are not walking in your purpose, because you are not walking in your power!"* That's when *my* circle of delay was broken.

Not with fireworks...but with a small, but obedient step, of washing my dishes.

Break the Loop Before It Becomes Your Legacy

You're not lazy. You're not unqualified. You're not behind. You're stuck in a pattern that's been spiritually tolerated, but must now be *broken*.

Blake called them 'mind-forged manacles', mental chains formed by fear and habit. And they must be shattered by obedience."

You were never meant to live in delay. You were meant to live in *divine timing*. And timing begins with *trust*.

Reflections

What have you started but not finished…and why?

_____

_____

What are your most common excuses for delay?

_____

_____

_____

What are you afraid will happen *when you actually succeed*?

_____

_____

_____

What is one thing you've been delaying, that you can commit to getting done today?

_____

_____

Declarations

I break the cycle of delay in my life...starting now.

My obedience is in motion. My destiny is not waiting.

I trust the timing of God...and I trust the power in me.

I walk in divine alignment. I am no longer available for delay.

Notes

_____

_____

_____

_____

_____

_____

_____

_____

Chapter Four
Boldness Is Not Arrogance

YOU ARE NOT BEING ARROGANT WHEN YOU MOVE LIKE YOU'VE BEEN SENT

There's a myth that has silenced too many *chosen* ones. That myth is that *confidence is arrogance*. That *boldness is pride*.

That, when you walk into a room, and own your presence, you're *doing too much*.

So you, *dim* your Light. You *defer*. You *shrink*. You *apologize* for taking up space.

I've been called arrogant, and I shrunk. I dimmed my light. I've been called a bully, and I was confused by it...*at the time*.

The truth is...walking in boldness is not arrogance, it's obedience.

Arrogance Centers *Self*... Boldness Centers *Assignment*

Arrogance says "look at *me*." Boldness says "look at *God* in me." There's a difference between self-promotion and divine expression. Arrogance pushes others down to lift itself up. Boldness *lifts the room* because it's powered by *purpose*. Arrogance boasts in what it knows, and in what it *thinks* it knows. Boldness speaks with authority because it *remembers who sent it*.

When God gives you a word, an assignment, a mantle...it is not *humility* to say 'oh, I'm just trying.' That is insecurity disguised as virtue and it delays impact. Goddard said "your word is your wand. What you declare with conviction becomes your world."

God Is Not Offended By Your Confidence

God is activated by your confidence. Hebrews 4:16 says... *"Let us then approach God's throne of grace with confidence..."*

Not timidity. Not reluctance. *Confidence.* When you walk in boldness, you are not putting yourself on a pedestal...you are standing on *assignment*. Your *hesitation* does not glorify God, your *obedience* does.

Breaking the Programming

So many of us were raised to be quiet. Be polite. Be strong...but don't be loud. And be dependable, but never disruptive. So when boldness rises in us, it feels *wrong*. It feels like rebellion. It feels like arrogance. But it's actually *the resurrection of identity*. You were taught to "wait your turn," but God is saying "This is your moment." You're not being rude. You're being *ready*.

Blake declared, 'Awake! Awake O sleeper… Expand!'

Boldness isn't rebellion. Your *spirit* already knows. It's your *soul* remembering who you are.

If They Call It Arrogance…Let Them

When you start walking in divine confidence, it will *offend the insecure*. Let it.

When you speak up, take the mic, claim your calling, and walk in favor – they'll whisper:

Who does she think she is?

She changed.

She doin' the most.

Let them!

And you can respond, in spirit…"I *know* who I AM…and I don't apologize for it."

Don't get distracted defending your boldness though.

Walk in it, and let the Fruit speak.

Jesus Was Bold…and They Hated Him For It

Jesus wasn't passive. He wasn't soft-spoken or scared. He flipped tables, called out hypocrites, spoke with authority, and unapologetically declared who He was. "Before Abraham was, I AM." (John 8:58)

They called it blasphemy. They plotted to kill Him. But He never apologized for being who He was sent to be. So why should you?

You're Not Arrogant...You're Activated

I've learned that the enemy does not mind a *humble* believer. He fears the bold one, because boldness unlocks doors. Boldness breaks cycles. Boldness silences shame. And for many of us, boldness is the healing we didn't know we needed.

When I finally started walking in my boldness...writing, teaching, speaking, showing up with my full voice...I didn't become arrogant.

I became *obedient*...I became *undeniable*...I became *free*.

Reflections

What moments from your past made you afraid to be bold?

_____

_____

_____

Whose opinions are you still *shrinking* for?

_____

_____

What assignment has God given you that requires a *bolder* you?

_____

_____

What's going to change when you stop apologizing for your power?

_____

_____

_____

Declarations

I am not arrogant...I am appointed.

I no longer shrink to soothe others. I rise to serve God.

Boldness is not rebellion. It is obedience in action.

I walk in divine confidence because I've been sent.

Notes

_____

_____

_____

_____

_____

_____

_____

_____

Chapter Five

Obedience Is the First Weapon

Before you cast out, bind up, or rebuke...have you obeyed?

Believers love the idea of *warfare*. Declaring. Binding. Loosing. Speaking in tongues.

And *yes*...those are powerful weapons.

But the most underrated, the most resisted, and *the most* powerful weapon you have is *obedience*.

Not flamboyance. Not titles. Not platform. *Obedience.*

Obedience doesn't get applause and it doesn't always make sense...to us. But it breaks things open in the spirit.

Obedience Before Strategy

We want strategy without surrender. We want God's outcomes without God's instructions.

We want to skip the quiet "yes" and go straight to the visible victory.

But God doesn't respond to noise. He responds to *obedience.*

"To obey is better than sacrifice." (1 Samuel 15:22)

Sometimes you're not under attack, you're just *out of alignment.*

We cry out for clarity. But God is saying: "I already spoke. Did you move?"

Delayed Obedience = Blocked Power

In Chapter 2, we called out the danger of *silence* after God speaks.

Now let's go a little deeper: delayed obedience is spiritual forfeiture.

Every time you delay...*the oil dries up. The window narrows.*

The opportunity shifts.

Obedience is not just about timing. It's about *access.*

"Imagination + Obedience = Manifestation" -Neville Goddard

Goddard taught that your *imagination* is divine instruction.

The *whispered* will of God revealed within.

"Faith is loyalty to the unseen reality."

He said that it's not enough to *imagine*. You must *assume and embody* the result.

That's *obedience* in action.

You can't affirm your power while disobeying your assignment.

To walk in divine manifestation, you must *become* what you've imagined in God.

Obedience Requires the *Mind* to Bow

We often make obedience a **body-level** act. But the real struggle is in the mind.

God says, "Do it." Your mind says...

What if I'm wrong?

What if they laugh? What if I mess this up?

But obedience is the moment when your spirit overrules your fear.

Blake's vision of human limitation was rooted in the mind: "I must create a system or be enslaved by another man's."

If you don't obey God's system, you will default to the world's.

Obedience Can Look Ordinary

I can tell you from experience…obedience doesn't always look supernatural.

Sometimes it looks like:

~ *Washing the dishes.*

~ *Writing that email.*

~ *Making that call.*

~ *Submitting that application.*

~ *Investing in yourself.*

~ *Finishing that thing you started.*

That night at my dining room table, when the Spirit said,

"THE DEVIL IS WINNING BECAUSE YOU'RE NOT WALKING IN YOUR POWER."

And...

"YOU ARE NOT WALKING IN YOUR <u>PURPOSE</u> BECAUSE YOU'RE NOT WALKING IN YOUR POWER."

It kept repeating itself...over...and over...and over...first at the table, then in my kitchen...and it continues to follow me, every time I don't move when I'm supposed to.

I didn't cast out a demon. But that night, I *did* wash every dish, pot, pan, and piece of silverware, in my line of vision, and I didn't feel tired.

That was spiritual warfare. *That was obedience.*

And *that* night, the *power* in my *spirit*, broke a cycle.

Obedience Will Cost You Comfort

Obedience is often uncomfortable because it disrupts the schedule *you* created.

The version of yourself you've grown accustomed to.

The people you've outgrown.

The safety nets you thought you needed.

But the *cost* of obedience will never outweigh the harvest of it.

You're asking God for miracles and at the same time, you're not moving when He tells you to.

Obedience Unlocks Power

When Abraham obeyed, a nation was born.

When Moses obeyed, the sea parted.

When Joshua obeyed, the walls fell.

When Jesus obeyed, death lost its hold.

What's waiting to be birthed, broken, or blessed, when *you obey?*

Reflections

What has God told you to do that you've hesitated on?

_____

_____

Where has your obedience been partial instead of complete?

_____

_____

_____

What "ordinary" task might actually be your spiritual weapon?

_____

_____

_____

What would immediately break open in your life if you obeyed?

_____

_____

_____

Declarations

Obedience is my weapon, and I use it without delay.

*My **yes** unlocks power, purpose, and peace.*

I silence my fears by obeying God.

I no longer negotiate with disobedience. I move when He speaks.

Notes

_____

_____

_____

_____

_____

_____

_____

_____

Chapter Six

Authority in Your Atmosphere

You don't just walk into rooms...you shift them

Some people enter a room and adapt to the atmosphere. They scan it. Gauge it. Then fit in.

When you're walking in divine power, you're not meant to *fit*...you're meant to *shift*.

"Where the Spirit of the Lord is, there is liberty, freedom." (2 Corinthians 3:17)

If the Spirit of the Lord is in *you*, liberty should follow you.

Chains should start loosening just because you walked in the room. Confusion should start breaking just because you opened your mouth.

This chapter is about you reclaiming your authority, and starting from right where you are...today!

You Are the Atmosphere

Too many believers still live like your *environment* has more *power* than your Spirit.

You are *not* called to be a thermometer. You are called to be a *thermostat*.

You don't report the temperature of a room; you *set it*.

This applies in your home, in your workplace, in your business, or in the middle of warfare.

You don't need a stage to carry authority. You need *alignment*.

What You Allow and What You Authorize

Every environment you enter asks two, silent, questions.

Will you take authority there, or will you come into agreement with what's *already* there?

Your answer is not found in your intention. Your answer is found in your posture.

Do you shrink when chaos rises? Do you go silent when dishonor shows up?

Do you join the complaining? The gossip? Or...

Do you speak peace? Do you pray...bind...rebuke? Do you shift the tone...without raising your voice?

Because what you allow, you authorize...and what you authorize, you empower.

The World Is Yourself "Pushed Out" -Neville Goddard

Goddard taught that "your world is the *outpicturing* of your inner reality".

"Your environment is your *imagination* made visible."

In other words:

What you believe inwardly, seeps into your atmosphere.

If you carry peace; peace is manifested.

If you carry chaos; chaos is manifested.

If you carry divine identity; divine identity is manifested.

Goddard's wisdom confirms this truth:

You don't need to fight for authority...you need to *embody* it.

The Prophet Within" -William Blake

Blake saw the *imagination* not just as mental creativity, but as a divine faculty. To him, *vision* is sacred. *Speech* is sacred. *Presence* is sacred.

In his work *"Jerusalem"*, he described spiritual men and women rising up to push back the fog of forgetfulness and declare:

"Awake, awake, O sleeper of the land of shadows."

To carry authority in your atmosphere is to *wake up to who you are*...and to wake others up too.

Atmospheres That Need Deliverance

To name a few...some spaces have been infected with:

~ *Emotional manipulation*

~ *Spiritual laziness*

~ *Fear*

~ *Gossip*

~ *Passivity*

~ *Abuse of power*

The reason these spirits maintain residence is because *no one* in the room will say, *"Not on my watch."*

You don't have to scream it.

But in your *spirit*, you must stake your ground.

In that very moment, you may not be able to change the room, but...you *can* refuse to changed *by* it *and* you can plant the seeds for reform.

Real Authority Is Felt Not Flaunted

Authority is not volume. It's not aggression. It's not spiritual intimidation.

Real authority is...

A quiet peace that unsettles chaos. Clear vision that confuses the enemy. Bold love that disarms attack.

Authority says..."This may be your territory right now...but I've been given jurisdiction, and this *thing* is about to change."

You Are a Walking Portal

When you walk into a room, with the Spirit of God inside you...

Heaven touches earth...*You carry the oil. You carry the keys. You carry the shift.*

If you forget that...you forfeit it.

Your authority is not in what you say. It's in what you *believe* and in what you *embody*.

And your atmosphere responds accordingly.

Reflections

What environments in your life feel wrong? Why?

_____

_____

Which areas in your life have you been shrinking from taking authority?

_____

_____

What would it look like to embody peace, purpose, and power in your spaces?

_____

_____

_____

What atmosphere has God assigned you to govern?

_____

_____

Declarations

I do not adapt...I shift.

I am the atmosphere. Wherever I go, God goes.

I walk in divine jurisdiction and refuse to authorize chaos.

My presence is not passive. It is prophetic.

Notes

___
___
___
___
___
___
___
___

Chapter Seven

The Devil Only Wins When You Withdraw

Your Absence Is His Strategy

Satan doesn't need to destroy you. He just needs you to *disengage*. To get tired.

To get discouraged. To get offended. To stop showing up. Stop praying. Stop leading. To withdraw.

Because when you *withdraw*, you...

~ Leave your post unguarded

~ Leave your gift unused

~ Leave your assignment unattended

The enemy isn't always trying to kill you. Sometimes, he's just trying to convince you to walk off the field on your own.

Absence as a Strategy

There is a spiritual cost to absence. Your presence is not optional, it's strategic. When you disappear, delay, or disconnect without divine release, you...

Stop the flow of wisdom

Interrupt the lineage of breakthrough

Give demonic systems room to breathe

And the devil celebrates every time you say:

~ *"I'm done."*

~ *"Let somebody else do it."*

~ *"I don't even care anymore."*

You need to know that when you withdraw, the devil doesn't just win the moment, he delays the movement.

Jesus Didn't Withdraw…He Advanced

Jesus rested. He retreated to pray. But He never **withdrew** from the assignment.

When they showed him that they hated Him. He knew they didn't understand.

And even when he knew that the cross loomed near...

~ *He showed up.*

~ *He taught.*

~ *He healed.*

~ *He finished.*

"For this purpose I came." (John 12:27)

You can't fulfill a divine purpose while you are hiding.

Withdrawal Is Self-Denial -Goddard *and* Blake

Goddard taught that *imagination* is divine action. Imagination is thinking, dreaming, hearing.

To *imagine* something and not act, is to *deny the -self*...

to "crucify your *I AM.*"

"You rise or fall by what you attach to I AM."

Blake warned of this too. In *"Jerusalem"*, he wrote of souls who gave up their divine inheritance and shrunk into darkness.

Not from sin, but from **apathy**.

Your power dies in withdrawal.

Your Light dims in disengagement.

Your assignment stalls when you stay silent.

You Show Up to Win

You don't show up because it's easy. You show up because it's *warfare*.

Every room you stand in, every gift you use, every truth you speak, pushes *darkness* back.

To the enemy, the most dangerous believer is the one who keeps showing up, even when the louder voice says, "Don't bother."

Reflections

Where in your life have you spiritually or emotionally withdrawn?

_____

_____

_____

What assignments have you quietly quit?

_____

_____

What would it take to re-engage with boldness and fire?

_____

_____

_____

What does "showing up" look like for you this season?

_____

_____

_____

Declarations

I do not withdraw...I advance...with authority.

My presence has purpose. My absence has cost.

I refuse to let discouragement cancel my destiny.

I show up, even when it's hard. Especially when it's hard.

Notes

_____

_____

_____

_____

_____

_____

_____

_____

Chapter Eight

Power Reclaimed...in Real Life

Spiritual authority looks like practical obedience

We know too well about reclaiming power *during* worship service. Often, that feeling is gone before you pull into your driveway.

We reclaim power during prayer, in affirmations, and in declarations. How long does that last? How long before that peace is disturbed?

When you truly reclaim your power, it looks like...saying *no* to what God did *not* assign to you.

When you truly reclaim your power, it looks like saying *yes* to what scares you, because it stretches you.

When you truly reclaim your power, you rewrite your daily patterns so that you can step into newness.

You cancel *agreements* with shame, because the debt has been paid. You starting your business, so He can show you what He can do.

You remove yourself from that toxic situation, because *you are enough*. Power reclamation is not just a feeling. It's a decision, it's a stand, *and* it's execution.

Power Is a Posture

You reclaim your power when...

You pray without begging, because you seek wisdom.

You speak up without apologizing, because you carry authority. Don't get it twisted! You're not loud, hostile, or aggressive. You don't need to be.

You plan without asking for permission, because God commissioned you. You take the risk without hesitation, because you trust Him.

Power is awareness, plus equipment, plus activation. Most of all, power is personal.

Stop looking around to see who's watching your transformation. It's not about them. It's about *you*.

Inner World First

Goddard taught that the outer world reflects the inner state.

To reclaim power outside, you must restore belief inside.

"Dare to believe in the reality of your assumption and watch the world play its part."

That means…if you assume you're weak, overlooked, too late…your life will give that to you.

But if you assume, stand on, *"I AM whole. I AM ready. I AM power,"* your life will give you that too.

Unlocking the Self

Blake's poetry often described the soul trapped in cycles of self-doubt. But he also saw the *awakening*…the soul tearing through illusion and reclaiming its place in the divine narrative. He called it **"building Jerusalem"**…restoring your sacred center.

And that's what reclaiming your power is. Rebuilding your temple, from the inside out.

Reflections

What area of your life feels powerless right now? Why?

_____

_____

_____

What is *one* action you can take this week to reclaim your authority?

_____

_____

What false identities have you agreed with that need to be revoked?

_____

_____

What would your day look like if you *embodied* power instead of waiting for something outside of yourself to move before you do?

_____

_____

_____

Declarations

I reclaim my voice, my time, my energy, and my fire.

My power doesn't need permission.

Every obedient step I take is warfare.

I walk in clarity, authority, and divine strength...daily.

Notes

_____

_____

_____

_____

_____

_____

_____

_____

Chapter Nine

The Awakening

You Are Not Available for Defeat

There is a moment in every believer's life when the enemy can no longer convince you that you are powerless.

It's not that life gets easier. It's that you are no longer *available for defeat*.

You recognize the game. You know who you are.

You've broken agreement with shame, silence, fear, and delay.

And now you live *awakened*.

Now, you walk in your power!

This Is the Awakening

It's not *just* emotional. It's not *just* spiritual. It's *practical*.

Awakening means...

You speak truth even when your voice trembles.

You pray like it matters.

You expect what you carry to shift things.

You walk into rooms like one who has been sent.

You put in the work, so you rest without guilt.

You've activated your assignment, and you are persistent.

You walk in your power!

"The New Self Emerges" -Neville Goddard

"Persist in the feeling of the wish fulfilled." -Goddard

When you truly believe that you've awakened, you live *from* that belief.

You no longer strive. You *embody*. You no longer beg. You *become*.

You walk in your power.

"The Rebuilder of Jerusalem" -William Blake

Blake saw the awakened soul as one who rebuilds the ruins.

A warrior. A builder. A poet. A prophet.

A human being who walks in divinity without apology.

"I will not cease from mental fight,

nor shall my sword sleep in my hand…"

Because once you're awake, you no longer ask, *"Am I worthy?"*

You ask, *"What's next?"*

You are walking in your power!

Reflection

What has shifted in your spirit since Chapter One?

_____

_____

_____

What are you no longer available for?

_____

_____

How has your voice, presence, or posture changed?

_____

_____

_____

What will you build, now that you've awakened?

_____

_____

_____

Declarations

I am no longer available for defeat.

I remember who I AM...and I act like it.

My awakened life is prophetic. My presence is power.

I walk as one who is sent, sealed, and unstoppable.

Notes

_____
_____
_____
_____
_____
_____
_____
_____

Thank You

If this message spoke to you, or helped to re-ignite something inside you, I would be honored if you would leave a review. And please, share this book with someone who needs it.

You can connect with me *and* find additional resources that support your walk in authority by visiting:
thepowerreclaimed.com

Your *journey* matters. Your *voice* matters. Your *power* has purpose.

About the Series

TO BE CONTINUED | BOOKS 2 & 3

Each book in *The Power Reclaimed* series is intentionally concise. These are not long reads, they are short activations. The goal is not more knowledge but more movement. Too often, we stall in cycles of consumption. These books are designed to spark action, not delay it. Read them. Live them. Walk in your power.

Book 2: You Are Not Walking in Your Purpose

Step into alignment with your God-given calling. You've awakened your power. Now it's time to bring it into focus. This book calls out the distractions, fears, and false assignments that keep you busy but not fruitful. Through scripture, lived experience, and prophetic insight, you'll learn to release what was never yours to carry and step boldly into the work God perfectly designed for you to do.

Book 3: You Forgot Who You Are

Return to your foundation...before the forgetting. This book is a prequel that takes you back to your wilderness seasons and hidden places where identity is forged. Through biblical reflection, personal insight, and spiritual recalibration, this short but potent read reveals how moments of silence, isolation, or obscurity are not evidence of abandonment -they are invitations to remember. To strip away false identities and reclaim your original design. This book helps you anchor your identity in truth so you can emerge whole, bold, and ready. Deeper revelation. Deeper activation.

About the author

Raine Cunningham is a writer, speaker, and visionary dedicated to helping others remember the divine power that lives within them.

Through her work, she speaks boldly to the wounded, the waiting, and the weary, calling you back to spiritual clarity and Kingdom identity.

This is her divine assignment... and *The Power Reclaimed* book series is just the beginning.

Beyond the pages, Raine continues her mission through **The Power Reclaimed Podcast**, where she walks listeners through real-life applications of each book and workbook.

On the website, **thepowerreclaimed.com**, readers can access her **blog** for ongoing insights, join the **Academy** for deeper teachings and skill-building courses, and explore a growing library of **resources for empowerment** designed to help you awaken, equip, and activate your God-given calling.

All of Raine's published works flow through **The Proverbial Seed Publishing**, a faith-driven imprint that serve as the primarily publishing house for the writings and testimonies of *The Power Reclaimed* community, a collective of voices rising in power, truth, and purpose.

Through every word she writes, every episode she records, and every resource she creates, Raine's heart is to see you fully reclaim what is yours.

www.ingramcontent.com/pod-product-compliance
Lightning Source LLC
Chambersburg PA
CBHW050917160426
43194CB00011B/2445